API

IIMN 2 0 2000

D1089108

Bender, Lionel
    Glacier / Lionel Bender. -- London ; New
York : Franklin Watts, c1988.

    32 p. : ill. ; bkl 3-5. -- (The story of
the earth.)   91763
    SUMMARY: Explains the formation, movement
and the melting of glaciers.
    ISBN 0-531-10647-0(lib.bdg.) : $11.90

                                      JUL 89

    1. Glaciers.   I. Title.   II. Series.

                                      88-50639

10-89

THE STORY OF THE EARTH
GLACIER

LIONEL BENDER

FRANKLIN WATTS
London · New York · Toronto · Sydney

© 1988 Franklin Watts

First published in Great Britain by
Franklin Watts
12a Golden Square
London W1

First published in the USA by
Franklin Watts Inc.
387 Park Avenue South
New York N.Y. 10016

First published in Australia by
Franklin Watts Australia
14 Mars Road
Lane Cove
NSW 2066

UK ISBN: 0 86313 738 5
USA ISBN: 0-531-10647-0
Library of Congress Catalog Card
No: 88-50369

Printed in Belgium

Consultant Dougal Dixon

Designed by Ben White

Picture research by Jan Croot

Illustrations:
Peter Bull Art

Photographs
GeoScience Features 1, 6, 7, 9, 11
    13, 17, 18, 21, 22, 23, 26
Alan Hutchinson Library 10, 19, 20
Survival Anglia 14, 29
Swiss National Tourist Office 16, 28
Wilderness Photographic Library 25, 31
ZEFA *cover*, 27

THE STORY OF THE EARTH
GLACIER

LIONEL BENDER

CONTENTS

This book tells the story of a typical glacier. A glacier is like a huge river of ice. It forms high up in the mountains where snow collects. Pressed down by its own weight, the snow turns to ice. Slowly the ice flows downhill, scraping away rocks from the ground underneath. The rocks stick to the ice and scour out a wide valley.

▽ The illustration shows the landscape features of the glacier. Snow that collects in rocky hollows on the mountain becomes packed into ice. Gradually the ice is crushed into a giant mass. It then starts to move downhill, rather like toothpaste being squeezed from a tube. When the ice reaches the warmer lowland, it melts.

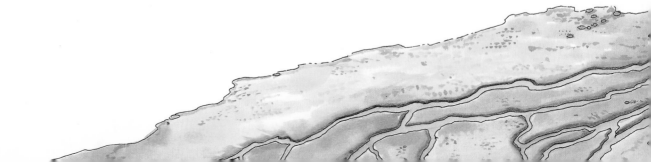

As the glacier moves downhill, the ice is pressed hard against the valley floor. Some of the bottom layer of ice melts. The meltwater helps the glacier slide down the mountainside. When the glacier flows around sharp bends in its valley, the ice cracks. Rubble carried along by the ice is dumped at the tip of the glacier.

▽The story of the glacier is divided into ten stages, as shown below. The following pages of the book look at each stage in turn. There are photographs of glaciers in different parts of the world. Diagrams explain how a glacier is formed and how it shapes the land as it flows from high mountain slopes to the lowland.

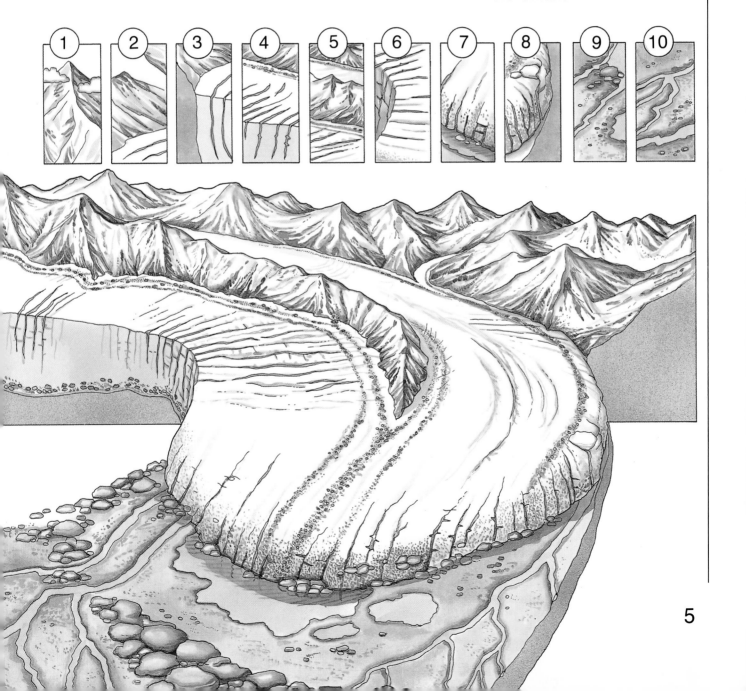

Winds blowing across the ocean pick up moisture. As the winds blow over the land, the moisture falls as rain. High up on the mountain, where it is very cold, the moisture forms ice instead. Tiny crystals of ice grow, and these join together in fluffy lumps that drift in the breeze.

These lumps of ice are snowflakes. The snowflakes are blown about by strong winds in a snowstorm or blizzard. Each blizzard covers the mountain slopes with fresh snow.

▷ The higher up a mountain you go, the colder the air becomes. Many mountains are so high that they always have a topping of snow, even in summer. This is the mountain El Misti in the Andes of Peru. It stands 5,822 m (19,200 ft) high. Snow often remains on the top of El Misti when the temperature on the lowland reaches 30°C (86°F) or more.

△ Snow does not lie firmly on a mountain slope. It often tumbles downhill in a large mass called an avalanche. The roaring force of an avalanche can carry away houses.

Snow lying in a shady hollow on the mountain does not melt, even in the warmth of the day. Each blizzard brings more snow, so that layer upon layer of snowflakes collect in the hollow. The weight of new snow on top crushes the bottom layers into a solid mass of ice.

We make snowballs in the same way, squeezing out the air from a handful of snow. The ice crystals melt and freeze again, forming a round, solid lump.

▷A snowfield on a mountainside in the Austrian Alps. It is dazzlingly white because air is trapped between the tiny ice crystals. Below the surface the snow is bluish because it has less air in it. Deep down in the snowfield there may be no air at all. Here the snow is a sea-blue solid mass of ice.

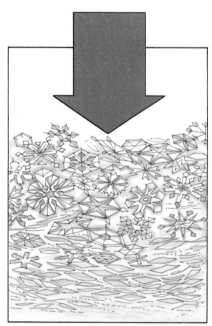

△Snow falls in an even layer. This first snow is light and fluffy and full of air. It is white and sparkles in the sun.

△More snow pushes down the lower layers. The ice crystals are squeezed into a mass called névé, or firn.

△In time, all the air is squeezed out of the névé and the snow becomes ice. The ice slowly moves downhill.

After a few months, or even years, the solid mass of ice becomes so heavy that it starts to move downhill. As it flows, it twists and bends along the valley. The glacier is born.

The movement of the ice widens and deepens the hollow on the mountainside. It forms a bowl-shaped valley called a cirque or corrie. The cirque is constantly being filled with snow. It cannot be seen until the glacier melts.

◁The slow downhill movement of this glacier in Norway has pulled the mass of ice away from the wall of the cirque. A huge crack has formed in the ice. This is called a bergschrund.

▽Once the ice mass moves out of the cirque, it becomes a real glacier. The glacier creeps slowly along its valley. It may not move more than a few feet a year.

The ice moves fastest in the middle of the glacier. The curved bands of grit on this glacier in France show where the ice is moving most quickly. This glacier is known as the Mer de Glace, which is French for the Sea of Ice.

The great weight and movement of the glacier wear away the land underneath. The rocks and rubble scraped and gouged out by the ice are carried along under the glacier. Their grinding action deepens and widens the valley.

Other rocks tumble down the valley sides and collect along the edges of the glacier. Some of these loose rocks fall down cracks in the surface of the glacier and become trapped within the ice. All the rocks, rubble and grit carried along by the glacier are known as moraine.

▷Mountain rock is always being worn down, or eroded, by wind, rain, rivers and frost. Glaciers are more powerful than any of these. A moving glacier cuts away the sides of its valley. The sides may then collapse on to the edges of the glacier. Since the glacier is always on the move, the loose rocks are carried away as moraine, as on this glacier in the French Alps.

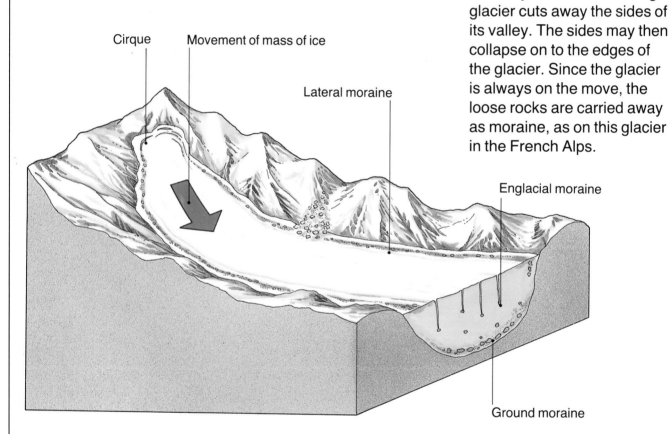

Cirque Movement of mass of ice

Lateral moraine

Englacial moraine

Ground moraine

△Rocks brought down by avalanches are carried along the edges of a glacier. They form side or lateral moraine. Rocks trapped in cracks in the ice form englacial moraine, meaning within the glacier. Rocks dragged along the valley floor by a glacier are known as ground moraine.

Glaciers and wildlife

The animals and plants that live close to glaciers are adapted to survive in the cold, windy conditions on mountains. Mountain goats, hares and marmots have thick warm coats. Eagles and other birds that feed on small animals can soar on the strong air currents. Flowering plants such as the edelweiss are small and low-growing to cope with the winds and frost. Their flowers bloom only in the warmth of spring.

▷Along an alpine glacier valley, tough grasses and heathers grow. Animals such as beetles, butterflies and ladybugs live on these few plants. The insects are eaten by spiders, which in turn are eaten by small birds. Larger animals such as mountain goats live on the steep slopes. Birds of prey such as the golden eagle soar above the glacier in search of food.

▽A lammergeier vulture nests on a narrow ledge high in the mountains. It feeds mainly on dead animals, but may also attack lambs, chickens and other farm animals.

Near the lowland, the glacier is joined by other glaciers from neighboring mountain slopes. Each mass of ice wears away its valley sides until only a ridge of rock separates the glaciers.

Eventually the ridge is worn away to a low, thin wall. The two glaciers then meet and flow into each other, creating one huge glacier. The loose rocks that had collected along the sides of the glaciers combine to form streaks of moraine all over the mass of ice.

▷A large glacier usually has dark streaks down the middle. They are formed as two glaciers flow into one another. The streaks are called medial moraine (medial means middle). The rocks and rubble that each has scraped away from the valley sides are combined into one mass. This is the Aletschgletscher, a glacier in Switzerland. It has lots of medial moraine.

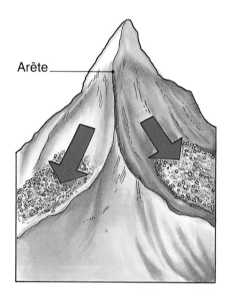

Arête

◁△On the Matterhorn in the Swiss Alps, glaciers have moved down the slopes and worn away the rock between them to form knife-edged ridges called arêtes.

Cracks and splits

As the glacier reaches flatter land, it moves along its valley more slowly than before. The great weight of ice keeps the bottom layers of the glacier flowing like toothpaste, and forces the whole mass toward lower ground.

The top layers of the glacier, however, are not under pressure and are still stiff and solid. They do not bend and flow like the lower layers. As a result, where the glacier turns corners and creeps over mounds in the valley, the top layers crack and split like glass.

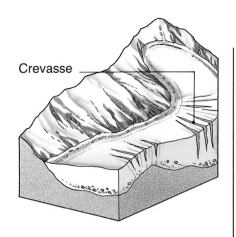

Crevasse

△ ▽ A glacier follows the bends and twists of its valley. When the glacier turns corners, its surface splits into deep cracks called crevasses. Other crevasses form as the center of the glacier moves ahead faster than the sides.

◁ The crevasses on the Lago Gelato Glacier in Italy have created jagged ridges of ice known as seracs. Crevasses and seracs often cut deep into the surface of the ice, forming a criss-cross pattern of cracks.

The glacier is now approaching warmer areas of land. The ice starts to melt. Puddles of water form on the surface of the glacier. Some of the water trickles away down crevasses, making streams and small rivers under the ice.

At the tip of the glacier all the ice is melting away. It melts most quickly along its sides and around big rocks buried in the ice. Here the glacier touches the valley walls and land heated up by the sun each day.

▽ The leading edge of a glacier looks like a thick tongue or flattened bulb of melting ice. The edge of this glacier in Norway is melting away. The meltwater has formed a stream and a shallow lake.

△ As the old surface ice starts to melt, the grit, rocks and rubble buried in the glacier are left lying on ice underneath. This is why the leading edge of a melting glacier usually looks very dirty. Its ice is gray, as here on a glacier near the River Rhone in Switzerland.

△Ground moraine covers the floor of this ice
cave in the Gross Glockner Glacier, Austria.

22

Ice caves and gorges

Each day, more and more ice melts on top of the glacier. Water is now trickling and tumbling through the glacier and flowing beneath it. Deep below the surface, the water is carving out a network of deep channels and caves. Within the caves huge icicles have formed – stalactites hanging from the roof and stalagmites reaching up from the floor.

▽ At the leading edge of this glacier in Italy, meltwater gushes out of a wide ice cave entrance. The water looks like milk because it is full of ground-up rock and rock dust, or "rock flour" from the moraine.

Over many years the climate gets warmer. The glacier melts farther and farther back up its valley. Along the way, it leaves behind all kinds of moraine. The loose rocks are spread all over the valley floor as layers of rubble and clay, hills and ridges, and as big boulders standing alone.

Eventually, these strange landscape features will be the only signs that the land was once covered by the glacier.

▷As a glacier moves downhill, it pushes along rocks and boulders in front of it. This end, or terminal, moraine is often made up of rocks carried hundreds of miles from where they first rested. When the glacier melts, the rocks are dumped on the ground.

▽A melting glacier may leave behind a curved ridge of moraine that marks where its front edge used to be. Meltwater streams may create winding ridges of grit as they dump tiny pieces of moraine.

The ridges are called eskers.
Mounds of sand and small stones dropped by the ice are called drumlins. Blocks of ice that melt may form hollows filled with water, which are known as kettle holes.

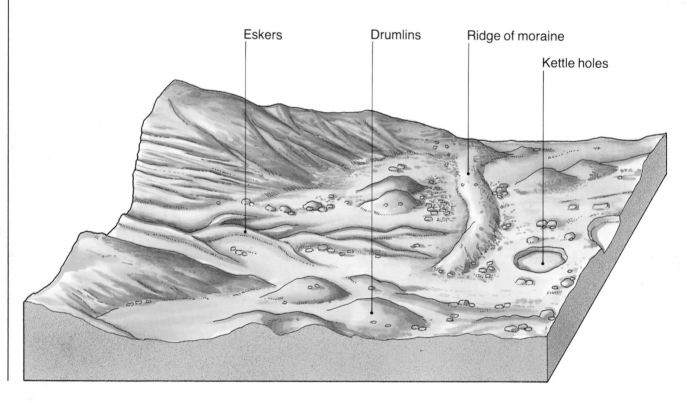

Eskers   Drumlins   Ridge of moraine

Kettle holes

The glacier has melted away, but there are clues to show us it was once there. Where it flowed over the lowland plain, the topsoil has been scraped off and carried away as moraine. The rocks on the plain have been worn smooth.

The scraping action of the glacier has widened and deepened the valley. The valley was once filled with a river, which carved out a V-shaped channel. The ice mass moving down the valley made the channel U-shaped.

▷In places, glacier valleys reach down to the sea. If the sea level rises after the glaciers have melted away, the U-shaped valleys fill with water, forming steep-sided inlets called fjords. There are many fjords like this one in Norway.

▷A valley that has been carved out by a glacier is clearly U-shaped, as this view along a valley near Zermatt in Switzerland shows.

Glaciers and people

Glaciers are of interest to such people as tourists, farmers and road builders. Glaciers are beautiful to look at. People travel from all over the world to visit them. The meltwater of a glacier often dumps rich soil on the land, which farmers can use to grow crops. Heaps of fine moraine, such as eskers and drumlins, are often full of sand and gravel that are useful for building highways and concrete bridges.

▽ Many hikers and walkers enjoy exploring glacial regions, like this one in the Jungfrau area of Switzerland. The meltwater lakes and the snow slopes near glaciers provide ideal sites for winter sports such as skiing and ice skating.

△ The constant movement of a glacier can be dangerous for people living in mountain areas. Where a glacier is perched on a mountain slope, like this one in Jasper National Park in Canada, any sudden movement of the ice mass could start off an avalanche of blocks of ice and moraine into the valley below.

Glossary

Arête A narrow razor-sharp ridge formed between two glaciers that join to form one big glacier lower down their valleys.

Avalanche A mass of snow, rock and, sometimes ice that slips down a mountainside, usually because snow on the lower slopes has melted away from beneath it.

Bergschrund A crack in the ice at the top of a glacier. It forms as movement of the mass of ice pulls the glacier away from the back wall of the mountain hollow in which the glacier was created.

Blizzard A snowstorm in which snowflakes are driven across a mountainside by strong winds.

Cirque A hollow on a mountainside where a glacier first formed. The hollow is shaped rather like an armchair. When the glacier has completely melted there may be a lake in the bottom of the cirque.

Corrie see **Cirque**

Crevasse A deep crack in the surface of a glacier. It is formed by the pressures and forces pulling apart the brittle ice of the topmost layers of the glacier.

Drumlin A mound of sand and gravel dumped on low ground by a melting glacier.

Esker A winding ridge of moraine formed by the meltwater streams flowing from a glacier.

Fjord A U-shaped valley, carved by a glacier, that has filled with seawater as the sea level rose.

Leading edge The tip (front end) of a glacier. If the ice is melting faster than the glacier is moving, the leading edge will retreat uphill. Otherwise, it constantly moves downhill.

Moraine Rubble, rocks, stones and grit ground away and pulled off the sides of a valley by a glacier. Moraine is carried along by the glacier and eventually dropped on the valley floor as the ice melts.

Névé A mass of snow that has become squeezed by the weight of snow above until it has almost formed solid ice.

Serac A tower of ice formed where networks of cracks in the ice, crevasses, cross one another.

Snow Moisture falling from the sky that freezes and forms clumps of tiny crystals of ice.

Facts about glaciers

Biggest glacier The continent of Antarctica is covered by an ice sheet that has layers of ice and moves over ground as one giant glacier. It measures 14 million sq km (5.4 million sq miles) and has an average thickness of 2,150 m (7,052 ft). It contains 99 percent of the ice on Earth.

The largest single "river of ice" type of glacier on Antarctica is the Lambert Glacier, which is 402 km (250 miles) long and 65 km (40 miles) wide.

Longest valley glacier The Siachen Glacier in the Karakorams in Mongolia, eastern Asia, is 76 km (47 miles) long. It joins up with the Hispar and Biafo glaciers to give a continuous length of ice of 122 km (76 miles).

Largest group of valley glaciers Apart from Greenland and Antarctic ice sheets, the glacier covering the largest area is the Malaspina Glacier in Alaska. It covers 2,176 sq km (840 sq miles). It is one giant glacier made up of several valley glaciers that flow together and spread across a lowland plain.

Fastest moving glacier The Quarayaq Glacier in Greenland moves at a speed of about 24 m (80 ft) a day. Most glaciers move much slower than this.

Longest fjord The longest drowned glacier valley is Nordwest Fjord, an inlet off the Scoresby Sund on the east coast of Greenland. It is 313 km (195 miles) long.

▷The Antarctic ice sheet is in places, several hundred feet thick. Where it meets the sea there are giant ice cliffs, like this one. Sometimes, part of the ice sheet breaks away to form floating platforms or blocks of ice. These are called ice floes and icebergs.

Index